A GIFT FROM ST. NICHOLAS

*The Story of Saint Nicholas
and a Special Christmas Letter*

By **Cristine Bolley**

Illustrated by **Bruce Eagle**

HONOR BOOKS

DEDICATED TO

Lindsey, Erin, Jamie, Jessica, and Kevin

and to all who still believe

MATTHEW 18: 5

A Gift from Saint Nicholas
ISBN 1-56292-774-4

Text copyright © 2001 by Cristine Bolley

Illustrations copyright © 2001 by Bruce Eagle

Conceptual design by Wings Unlimited
P.O. Box 691532 • Tulsa, OK 74169-1532

Published by Honor Books
P.O. Box 55388 • Tulsa, Oklahoma 74155

Book design by Koechel Peterson & Associates

Unless otherwise indicated, all Scripture quotations are taken from the *King James Version* of the Bible.

Scripture quotation marked NIV are taken from the *Holy Bible, New International Version*®. Copyright © 1973, 1978, 1984 by International Bible Society. Used by permission of Zondervan Publishing House. All rights reserved.

HAVE YOU ALWAYS WANTED to know who the real Santa Claus is? My daughters once thought that I was Santa Claus, but he has been visiting homes on Christmas Eve for about 1600 years! And I'm not quite *that* old. So, off to the library we went searching for the history of this jolly, old celebrant of Christmas. Here's what we found.

The first Santa Claus was a real person named St. Nicholas. He lived sometime between the third and fourth centuries. Stories about his generous deeds were retold so many times that some tales grew into legends. The people of Russia said he had reindeer; the Scandinavians said he lived in the snow; the Dutch were first to call him Santa Claus; and the Americans painted him as an overweight, bearded man in a red and white suit. But the real St. Nicholas wore the robe of a priest.

At the young age of nineteen, Nicholas became the bishop of a church in Myra, a land of "green hills, warm sun, and soft sea breezes" in the country now known as Turkey. He was probably thin because he observed the prayer and fasting days of the church. According to the history books, many miracles have been recorded as a result of this bishop's prayers.

St. Nicholas understood that life's real treasure is found in doing what is right in the eyes of God, and he discovered that joyful peace comes from loving others. He is remembered fondly for his anonymous efforts to give away his inherited wealth.

Most certainly, St. Nicholas never meant to become the icon of Christmas, but his passion to give to others in response to God's greatest gift—His only Son—is what this holiday is all about. This letter from St. Nicholas calls us to put our hope in the real Star of Christmas—giving us Someone to believe in, after all . . .

ear children of all sizes,
        from all nations near and far,
I hope you will remember
        to watch for the Christmas star.

You'll see it shining brightly
        in the sky on Christmas Eve,
a night of hope-filled miracles
        for those who will believe.

For when you see the Christmas star,
        you know the time is near
to celebrate the joyous day
        when Jesus first brought cheer.

MATTHEW 2:10

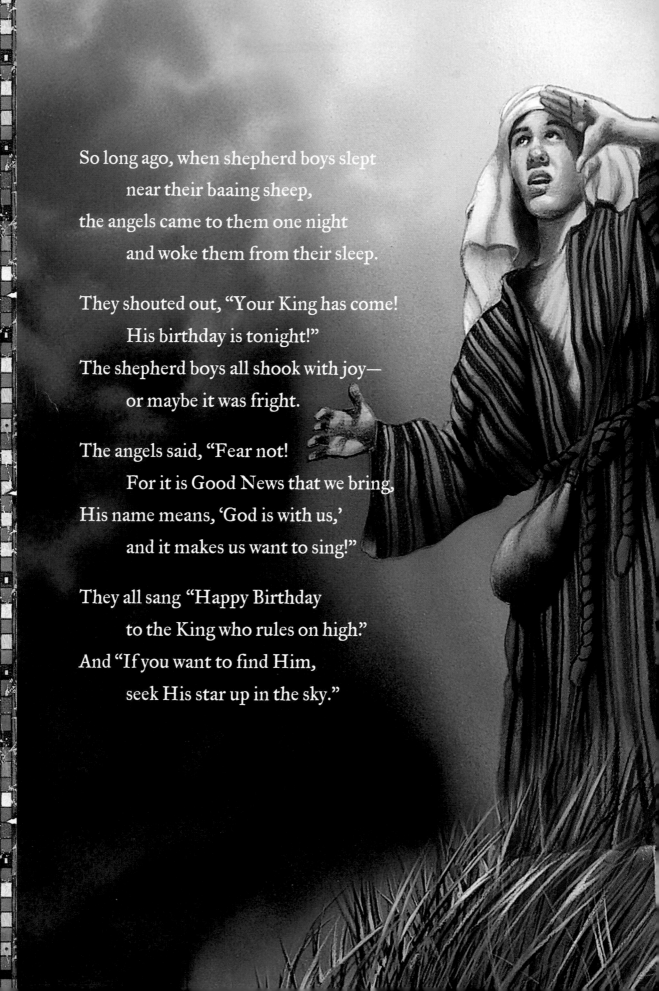

So long ago, when shepherd boys slept
        near their baaing sheep,
the angels came to them one night
        and woke them from their sleep.

They shouted out, "Your King has come!
        His birthday is tonight!"
The shepherd boys all shook with joy—
        or maybe it was fright.

The angels said, "Fear not!
        For it is Good News that we bring,
His name means, 'God is with us,'
        and it makes us want to sing!"

They all sang "Happy Birthday
        to the King who rules on high."
And "If you want to find Him,
        seek His star up in the sky."

Luke 2:11

The shepherds knew they'd found Him
when the star grew very bright.
They found the Holy Babe
tucked in by Mary's side that night.

They worshiped Him, our Savior,
though it seemed a little odd
that this tiny, Baby Jesus
could lead them back to God.

MATTHEW 1:21

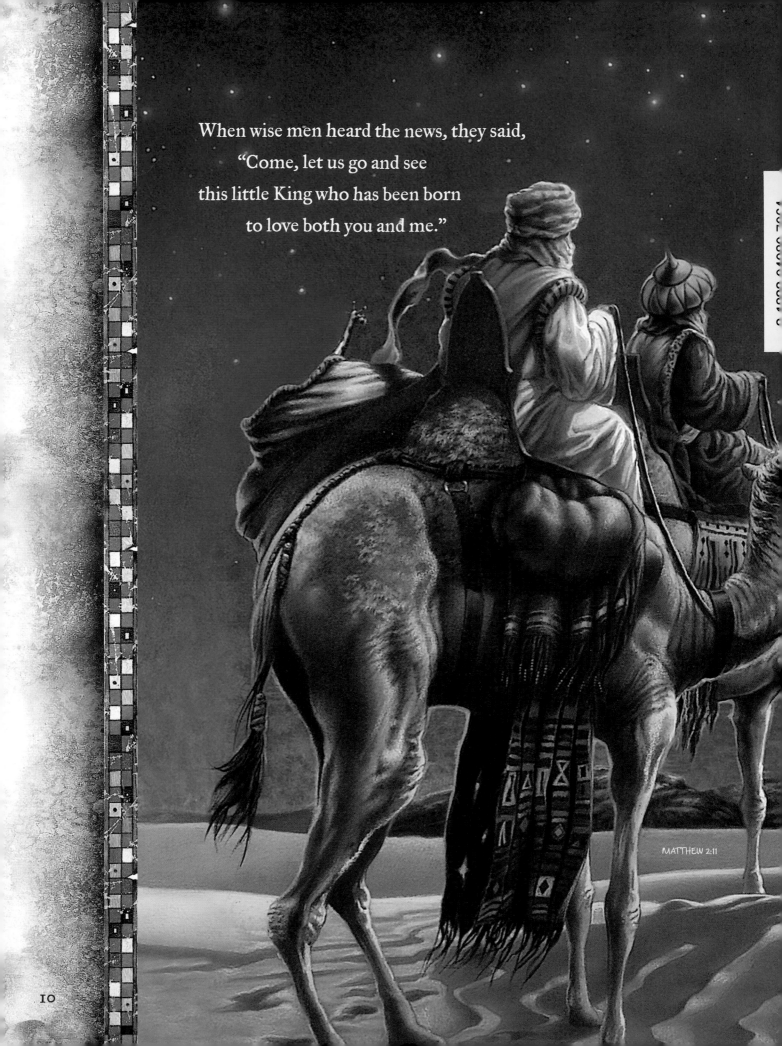

When wise men heard the news, they said,
    "Come, let us go and see
  this little King who has been born
    to love both you and me."

MATTHEW 2:11

IO

They put their gifts on camels' backs
and traveled very far
to see the newborn baby Boy
who slept beneath the star.

The little King grew up and taught
"In God, we must believe."
And said that it is better to give gifts
than to receive.

I get so many letters
at this time of every year,
from children all around the world—
their questions are so dear!

"Dear Santa Claus" they begin,
	"Father Christmas, or St. Nick,
Père Noël, Kriss Kringle, Sinterklaas—
	please answer quick!"

"I'm hoping for a present.
	Can you tell me if it's true?
My gifts on Christmas morning,
	do they really come from you?"

"It doesn't seem too likely,"
	wrote a little girl named Ruth,
"I'm nearly ten and old enough
	to hear the grown-up truth!"

Santa
is in!

JOHN 16:24

13

Be careful with your questions,
        lest you get the wrong reply;
instead of asking who brings gifts,
        perhaps you might ask why.

To solve the puzzle of the gifts
        beneath your Christmas tree,
you'll need to know the tale of why
        the gifts are giv'n from me.

JOHN 8:32

14

I saw the ones who'd lost their hope,
   and prayed to find a way
to help them know the hope and joy
   of that first Christmas day.

And then I had a vivid dream,
   which lives in mem'ry still,
of people giving presents
   to their neighbors with goodwill.

I dreamed that I saw Jesus,
    sitting by the throne of God.
He smiled at me, but overwhelmed,
    I could but give a nod.

"Oh, Nicholas," He said to me,
    "I'm glad that you are here.
For you can help me very much
    by spreading Christmas cheer.

"My birthday is tomorrow,
    and I have a fun-filled plan.
What say we have a party
    for each woman, child, and man?

"Instead of lovely presents
    that you bring to honor me,
give gifts of joy to girls and boys
    and everyone you see.

"So all will know My promises
    most certainly are true.
But these first gifts, dear Nicholas,
    will have to come from you.

"By giving gifts to children,
    the grownups will surely see,
their heart's desire will come to them
    when they delight in Me.

PSALMS 37:4

"Yes, that's what we must do," He said.
   "Let's start right now—today!
Go and find the favorite things
   with which most children play.

"Tomorrow on My birthday,
   please be sure to spread My joy,
and leave a special present
   for each precious girl and boy."

I could not understand
   what He had asked for me to do.
I stammered and I said, "Oh, Lord,
   I do not have a clue!"

I knelt and thanked my Father God
   For all His love and care,
and all at once I felt His love
   fill up the midnight air.

I asked Him where and how to find
   so many wondrous gifts,
and even speculated that this plan
   might start some myth.

As soon as I had spoken,
   I saw clearly in His eyes
my doubt and hesitation
   did not catch Him by surprise.

He smiled and said, "Just trust Me, Nick,
you needn't make such noise,
I multiplied the fishes—
I can do the same with toys.

"And I will bless such giving."
Jesus looked at me and smiled.
"I'll bless all those who give to folks
in manner meek and mild.

"It'll be the best of parties;
I want everyone to come.
They'll give to one another.
Just imagine all the fun!"

Then, suddenly, I sat up straight
and woke with joyful heart.
I knew precisely what to do
and couldn't wait to start.

I hurried to my kitchen
to prepare some tasty snacks,
and there I found my childhood toys
stuffed in a flour sack!

MATTHEW 14: 19-21

22

I thought about the boy
   who gave to Jesus his few fish,
I knew right then that I could give
   my Lord His birthday wish.

If He could feed five-thousand men
   with but a meager meal,
I knew that He could use my toys
   to show His love is real.

23

I dressed up in my best disguise
and waited until night,
then took my gifts to children dear,
and hurried out of sight.

MATTHEW 6:3-4

The children were not meant to think
    the gifts had come from me;
the gifts were meant as evidence,
    God's love is plain to see.

Jesus is the Star of Christmas—
    a brilliant Star He is,
for giving gifts was not my thought,
    the credit all is His!

That Jesus loves all people,
    He wants everyone to know;
His birthday celebration
    is one way He tells us so.

He said that if we give good gifts
    to others who have needs,
that He'll return good gifts to us,
    like harvest from our seeds.

And when we give in secret,
    not expecting in return,
rewards will be far greater
    than if gain we tried to earn.

And so on every Christmas Eve,
    the story goes (and grows!),
that I will sneak into your house.
    But how? Still no one knows!

That I will also leave a gift
    before I disappear.
But now the truth of Christmas gifts
    should be so crystal clear.

MATTHEW 6:33

29

ACTS 20:35

A gift to you from Santa Claus
was given just to say,
the greatest joy comes back to you
when you give joy away!

Love,
Saint Nicholas

Did you find the hidden Bible references in each picture?

Read these verses to learn more about Christmas.

Did you find Matthew 18:5 NIV on page 2 or 3?
Jesus said, "Whoever welcomes a little child like
this in my name welcomes me."

Did you find Matthew 2:10 on page 4 or 5?
The Bible says, "When they [the wise men] saw
the star, they rejoiced with exceeding great joy."

Did you find Luke 2:11 on page 6 or 7?
The angels said, "For unto you is born this day
in the city of David a Saviour, which is Christ
the Lord."

Did you find Matthew 1:21 on page 8 or 9?
The angel of the Lord said to Joseph, "She [Mary]
shall bring forth a son, and thou shalt
call his name JESUS: for he shall save his
people from their sins."

Did you find Matthew 2:11 on page 10 or 11?
The Bible says, "they saw the young child with
Mary his mother, and fell down, and worshipped
him: and when they had opened their treasures,
they presented unto him gifts; gold, and
frankincense, and myrrh."

Did you find John 16:24 NIV on page 12 or 13?
Jesus said, "Until now you have not asked for
anything in my name. Ask and you will receive,
and your joy will be complete."

Did you find John 8:32 on page 14 or 15?
Jesus said, "Ye shall know the truth, and the truth
shall make you free."

Did you find Proverbs 29:18 on page 16 or 17?
The Bible says, "Where there is no vision, the people
perish."

Did you find Psalm 37:4 on page 18 or 19?
The Bible says, "Delight thyself also in the LORD;
and he shall give thee the desires of thine heart."

Did you find James 1:17 NIV on page 20 or 21?
The Bible teaches, "Every good and perfect gift
is from above, coming down from the Father of
the heavenly lights, who does not change like
shifting shadows."

Did you find Matthew 14:19-21 on page 22 or 23?
The Bible tells the story about Jesus feeding
thousands of people with just two fish! "He
commanded the multitude to sit down on the grass,
and took the five loaves, and the two fishes, and
looking up to heaven, he blessed, and brake, and
gave the loaves to his disciples, and the disciples
to the multitude. And they did all eat, and were
filled: and they took up of the fragments that remained
twelve baskets full. And they that had eaten were
about five thousand men, beside women and
children."

Did you find Matthew 6:3-4 NIV on page 24 or 25?
Jesus said, "When you give to the needy, do not let
your left hand know what your right hand is doing,
so that your giving may be in secret. Then your
Father, who sees what is done in secret, will reward
you."

Did you find Luke 6:38 NIV on page 26 or 27?
Jesus said, "Give, and it will be given to you. A
good measure, pressed down, shaken together and
running over, will be poured into your lap. For with
the measure you use, it will be measured to you."

Did you find Matthew 6:33 on page 28 or 29?
Jesus said, "Seek ye first the kingdom of God, and
his righteousness; and all these things shall be added
unto you."

Did you find Acts 20:35 on page 30 or 31?
The Bible says, "Remember the words of the Lord
Jesus, how he said, It is more blessed to give than
to receive."

Additional copies of this book are
available from your local bookstore.

If you have enjoyed this book, or if it
has impacted your life, we would like to
hear from you. Please contact us at:

HONOR BOOKS
Department E
P.O. Box 55388
Tulsa, Oklahoma 74155
Or by e-mail: info@honorbooks.com